# Casket

*Also by Andy Brown*

# Andy Brown

# Casket

Shearsman Books

First published in the United Kingdom in 2019 by
Shearsman Books
50 Westons Hill Drive
Emersons Green
BRISTOL
BS16 7DF

www.shearsman.com

ISBN 978-1-84861-683-7

*With many thanks to James Simpson, Marc Woodward,
Kelvin Corcoran and Rob Magnuson Smith, who listened
generously to drafts of these poems*

*The poem titles in this volume are in the Northumbria font, which was
modelled on original 7th and 8th century monastic gospel books from
Northern England.*

*The runes are in Babelstone Runic Beowulf.*

# CASKET

The Franks Casket (or Auzon Casket) is an 8th century Anglo-Saxon treasure chest, donated to the British Museum by a private owner from Auzon, France. Made from whalebone, the front, back, sides and lid of this small chest are decorated with runic inscriptions, some Latin text and images from various religious and mythical traditions.

Runes comprised the earliest Germanic script, derived from earlier alphabets and modified into angular forms so that they could be carved. Each rune has an equivalent letter in the Latin alphabet, allowing for Anglo-Saxon and modern English translations. Each rune also has a pictorial value: for example, in the runic ᚠᛁᛋᚳ ('fisc'), f signifies 'wealth', i 'ice', s 'sun' and c 'torch', yielding a sequence of four images. To write the following poems, I determined the sequence of images yielded by each runic word and then used these images, or variants of them, to write the poems.

A table of all the runes in the Anglo-Saxon Futhark alphabet follows, showing their equivalent English letters and their pictorial values. In their esoteric sense, runes came to symbolize something mysterious and difficult to interpret – the word 'rune' translates as 'mystery', as well as 'letter', 'row' and 'series'. It may also derive from the Germanic word 'runo', meaning 'a song'.

Using this multilevel technique of 'translation', the following poems are an attempt to capture something of the layered histories, from ancient times to present, of the place where I now live: the river Teign and its surrounding area.

*'open the box, a knucklebone of tin'*
Kelvin Corcoran, 'Pytheas'

## The Anglo-Saxon Futhark Alphabet

| ᚠ | ᚢ | ᚦ | ᚩ | ᚱ | ᚳ | ᚷ |
|---|---|---|---|---|---|---|
| feoh - f | ur-u | þorn - þ | os - o | rad -r | cen - c | ʒiefu - z |
| "wealth" | "cattle" | "thorn" | "mouth" | "ride" | "torch" | "gift" |

| ᚹ | ᚺ | ᚾ | ᛁ | ᛄ | ᛇ | ᛈ |
|---|---|---|---|---|---|---|
| pynn - p | haeʒl - h | nyd - n | is - i | jear - j | eeoh - eo | peorđ -p |
| "joy" | "hail" | "need" | "ice" | "year" | "yew" | "game" |

| ᛉ | ᛋ | ᛏ | ᛒ | ᛖ | ᛗ |
|---|---|---|---|---|---|
| eolxecʒ - x | siʒel - s | tyr - t | beorc - b | eoh - e | man - m |
| "elk-sedge" | "sun" | "Tyr" | "birch" | "horse" | "man" |

| ᛚ | ᛜ | ᛟ | ᛞ | ᚪ | ᚫ | ᚣ |
|---|---|---|---|---|---|---|
| lagu -l | ing - n | œđl - œ | dæz - d | ac - a | æsc - æ | yr - y |
| "lake" | "Ing" | "estate" | "day" | "oak" | "ash" | "bow" |

| ᛠ | ᛡ | ᛣ | ᛢ | ᚸ | ᛤ | ᛥ |
|---|---|---|---|---|---|---|
| ear - ea | iar - ia | kalc - k | kalc - kk | gar - g | cpeorđ - cp | stan - st |
| "earth" | "serpent" | "chalice" | | "spear" | "fire" | "stone" |

7

## I. Whalebone

*(front panel)*

ᚠᛁᛋᚳᚠᛚᚩᛞᚢᚪᚻᚩᚠᚩᚾᚠᛖᚱᚷ | ᛗᛖᛒᛖᚱᛁᚷ | ᚹᚪᚱᛈᚷᚪᚱ:

ᚷᚱᛁᚻᚷᚱᚩᚱᚾᚦᚪᚱᚻᛖᚩᚾᚷᚱᛖᚢᛏᚷᛁᛋᚹᚩᛗ | ᚻᚱᚩᚾᛖᛋ

*Fisc flodu ahof on fergen-berig*
*Warþ gas-ric grorn þær he on greut giswom.*
      *Hronæs ban.*


The fish stirred up the flood    on to the mountainous cliff;
The king of terror saddened    when he swam onto the shingle.
      Whalebone.


From the river's curved calligraphy
We haul up a trawl-net of treasures
And tip the shells out on the sorting rack…
Dark mussels fall in clattering cascades.

This unforgiving trade, when the ice
Of February frets the core and fingers
And the sun's declining disk smoulders,
Barely bright enough to light the creek,

Although it shimmers on the shellfish
And brings the silted backwater to life
As it trickles out at Netherton Bridge
Towards the estuary's open mouth.

Daylight sketches the flanks of piebald stock
Grazing placidly where aurochs once roamed,
Protected from the squalls beneath banked oaks
That shelter them from hail and cutting sleet

As they slowly turn their ruminative mouths
To the business of turning pasture into gold.
    *God gives us seven hungry mouths to feed,*
    *But winter's only shrunken guts and worry.*


*


Along the seafront, the wealthy promenade
Watching the hale take their horses for a ride.
The ailing fill their lungs with healing air,
Stopping to read the illustrated text
Where the old harpoon lies stored
Under glass in its heritage box –

    *From here the township's whalers set to sea*
    *In eighteen hundred and twenty nine, never to return...*


In the amusement arcade along the pier
Children shovel coins into the horse races,
Betting pocket money on mechanics
Tuppence at a time, their faces turning hope
To profit and loss beneath the neon lights.

Under slender birches on the esplanade
A sideshow donkey champs in its nosebag
Outside the pound shops and boarded-up hotel –
    *Someone here's been taken for a ride –*
While in the shallow rock pools of the bay
An Anglo-Saxon breaks the frazil ice,
Draws up a flounder with a well-aimed spear.
    With mouths to feed, the fish brings untold joy.

Upstream, the cattle underneath the oaks
Disinterestedly watch a water skier ride

The estuary, carving her hieratic V
As though some blade had slashed the water's skin.

In the boatyard the oak planks mature,
Furnishing the whaling fleet with boats
To comb Imperial waters heading north,
Bearing the national torch in pursuit
Of the great ocean gods; coursing waves
To feed the lamps back home...

> *The leviathan feels the thorn lodged in her side,*
> *Buried in her blubber – like towing a tree.*
> *She takes that oaken vessel for a ride.*
> *Here at sea*
> *The hail falls fast on seahorse and sailor alike*
> *From the mouth of god. Each soul and sailor*
> *Hungry in their need.*

Beneath the lamps on the sea wall, a tourist
Spears the contents of a carton of whelks
With the languid strokes of a weekend away.
Behind her, the kids spin scooters and boards
Over the humps of the concrete skate park,
Ditching their rides to glut themselves
On teetering ice creams beneath the placard
Of the plastic cow who sings the praise of dairy.

On the beach they haul the speared whale
Through the ice-cold surf. Their faces are lit
With the light of god. Their mouths proclaim
The light of man... *Hail the great whale!*

Above the beach, the car park empties out
As visitors drive home, their own mouths open

To the spectacle of sunset.

                        *What more could you need?*
On their long slow climb from the valley,
They watch the ash trees slowly turn to flame
In the sun's reaching rays.

                        Back downstream
The mussel men throw their bushel baskets
Of woven willow and birch across their backs,
As strong as the oaks that line the banks…
  *The river yields enough for all our needs.*

## II. Two Brothers
*(left side panel)*

ᚱᛖᛗᚹᛖᛚᚢᛋᚱᛖᚢᛗᚹᚨᛚᚢᛋᛏᚹᛇᚷᛖᚾ ᛁ ᚷᛁᛒᚱᚩᚦᚨᚱ

ᚨᚠᛇᛞᛞᚨᚻᛁᛇᚹᚣᛚᛁᚠᚱᚩᛗᚨᚳᚨᛋᛏᚱᛁ ᚩᚦᛚᚨᚢᚾᚾᛖᚷ

*Romwalus Reumwalus,     twægen gibroþær,*
*afædda hia wylif Romæcæstri,*
*oþla unneg.*

*Romulus and Remus, two brothers,*
*were nourished by a she-wolf in Rome,*
*far from their native land.*


A white horse gallops across the hill
Incised into the semblance of a god,
Or just the joyful signature of man,
Enduring longer than the oaks by the lake
Where a herd of cattle comes to drink the sun.

To reach the present day, dig deep
Through the level berm that runs above
The ditch and counterscarp of Castle Dyke
Here on top of Little Haldon Hill
Above the steep cut of Smallacombe Goyle:
  A stocking pen, a single line of earthworks,
    A redistribution centre and food bank,
      Place of refuge and permanent settlement.

Cross the wooden boardwalk that cuts through
The simple gateway set into the ramparts
And find there, a stone's throw to the east,
Two barrows, two burial mounds,
Where *the corn-bearing earth* holds two brothers...

\*


Romulus and Remus suckled by a she-wolf;
Or Castor *the bold* and Pollux *the boxer*,
Who each take turn to live and die
Through one day's plotline to the next,

Prisoners of the fertile earth;
Or Hengist *the stallion* and Horsa *the horse* –
Outcast travellers, twins, who led a people
And forged this kingdom... *Rule Brittania.*

\*


Above the estuary on the lowland heath,
With its car parks, picnic spots and trodden paths,
A hunter lets the passing thought of 'farmer'
Leave his lips, burning back heather and gorse

Where a researcher comes to toss her quadrat
Among the climbing *corydalis* white
And *dodder* which creeps across its host
In a scribbled snarl of red string.

She counts the Nightjar and Stonechat
Competing for nest sites with Yellowhammer;
Notes the movements of adder and lizard
Sunning themselves where the vixen hunts

And where the braying redcoat hunters come,
Like mounted *Dioscuri*, their spears aloft,
Running down the aurochs and the fox
Between the oaks at the side of the lake

Where the cattle have come to drink the sun.

\*


A walk is its own form of glory;
Brings you into the moment
Of the field – its spears of rush
Growing through hummocks of horse dung.

There's no need to hurry; stoop
And pick up something half-seen –
Lying hidden by hoarfrost in the rides
Underneath the birch trees and the ash:

A napped-flint arrowhead sung from the mouth
Of the heath where the white horse rides.

\*


Under the emblem of the oak leaf,
The *National Trust* collection box stores coin
For the upkeep of the estate. Day after day
The visitors come to see the last few ash trees
Before they finally disappear for good,
Wiped out by a fungus, like Autumn
Brought to a close in storms of hail and ice.

*English Ash Trees Resistant to Dieback*
Some posters round the grounds announce

And yes, give thanks, for some still bow
Their limbs by the lake, shedding
Hopeful seed and ice-white pollen –
Their stored-up treasure; their future.

\*

From the valley the motocross riders
Contest the peace of the commons;

Each circuit declares their right to the land;
Bearing their light through the trees. On the heath

The sun turns the bunchgrass to glory.
A buzzard rides invisible thermals of air.

Beneath the ground, the sleeping roots whisper
Of how the looming ice age lies in wait.

\*

Of two brothers, one always has the louder voice.
One is the thorn.

One's body is burned on a boat
On a lake and turned to ash.

One is the ox. One has a burning wish.
What both need is a horse and spear –

To forge a nation's voice on Haldon Hill
Above the steep cut of Smallacombe Goyle.

## III. homestead

ᚠᚷᛁᛚ

*Ægili*

*Egil (the archer)*


Up at the allotments,
   The circle of ash
     From the fire we held
       Last autumn    scars the ground.
     Spears of new growth lie
   Locked in frost and ice.
The water butt is solid.

I dig up leeks, cut chard,
   Mulch artichokes and rhubarb,
     Then drive off for the packaged staples
       That lie in public stockpiles
     Beneath the supermarket sign…
   *We'll see this besieged homestead*
*Through til spring.*

## IV. The City

*(rear panel, which bears a mix of runes and Latin words)*

ᚺᛖᚱᛖᚠᛖᚷᛏᚪᚦ ᛏᛁᛏᚢᛗᛖᚾᚷᛁᚢᚦᛖᚢ

hicfugianthierusalim ᚪᚠᛁᛏᚪᛏᛟᚱᛖᛋ ᚺᛖᛗ ᚷᛁᛋᛚ


*her fegtaþ titus giuþeasu*
*hic fugiant hierusalim afitatores*
*dom / gisl*

*Here Titus fights the Jews:*
*here the inhabitants flee Jerusalem.*
*doom / hostage*


At distant Holwell
The miners hammer
Their feathers and tares
Into the stress lines
Of obdurate rock

Come rainstorm or hail.
The boulders fracture
While empty hoppers
Wait on the tracks of
The granite tramway

Its channels chiselled
To pilot the wheels
Of the loaded trams
Drawn up by horses
Twenty to a train

Over to Stover
Some ten miles distant
Down the Templar Way
Through old Yarner Wood
Across Chapple Bridge

And the Bovey Leat
Unpacked at Teigngrace
Conveyed by canal
To Teignmouth's New Quay
Bound for the City

*Giant* and *Blue* granite
For the GPO
British Museum
London's bridge rebuilt
All hungry for stone…

\*

…From where rides-in the fair boy Keats,
Penning tubercular verse *in pleasant darkness*,

And an old man sitting at a library PC
Who looks the spit of Charles Babbage,
Stabbing the keys while he searches the Web

For Donald Crowhurst, *farewell farewell*,
As his vessel, the *Teignmouth Electron*, begins
To tackle the race, the Golden Globe,
On its single-handed quest for glory;

And here comes Fanny Burney
In all her bathing-suited splendour,

Dipping in our township's icy waves
From the boards of her bathing machine,

While Joseph Mallord William Turner
Adds touches of grandeur to his canvas –
A sunset upstream of the quays –

Colouring the cattle who graze the saltings
With the liquid gold of sky and foreshore.

*

*Open the box* – a carved knucklebone
Of horse; ornate jewels, brooches, buckles
And metal hasps as intricate as day.

*Notae* scored on footmen's spears,
Swords, shields, shafts and bosses;
Statuettes stock-still as ice.

Tablets of wood inscribed with thorns;
Stirrups, tools and ladies' combs;
Amulets of wood and bone.
Symbolic rings that whisper of the sun.

Finely etched *fibulae* of cattle.
Drinking horns. Pigmented mysteries
Painted on small cuts of cow hide –
All stored inside this scrimshawed ivory.

*

And now the snow crust has begun to melt
Along the sodden link road verge

The bodies of badgers and deer – dazzled
And struck by the lights of luxury cars –

Emerge through the grey slush,
Like the bodies of the Britons and the Saxons

Who died here in battle on Haldon Hill
Where the oxen grazed among their fallen spears.

\*


*Open the box* on talismanic objects portable
And all their worldly kind –

The Thames Scramsax;
The yew box of Garbole;

The golden pin of Aquincum;
The glorious Meldorf brooch;

The Torque of Pietroassa
That hails the mother goddess,

Regeneration and fertility
And crop-bringing rains on the runestave;

The icy blade of Dahmsdorf…
Made and lost and found and lost again,

Ephemeral as emojis
On the screen of a mobile phone.

\*

And walking home on darkened pavements
Bletted by the fallen leaves of winter,

Passing underneath graffiti'd roadsigns,
The underground streams of this riven township

Murmur of themselves: the East
And West side divvied by the Tame

Now running solely in culverts
Underneath the slabs and tarmac

From Brimley Brook through the swollen
Winterbourne, after winter's spate.

\*

Now the season is shifting,
The spun-out debris
Of windblown oak trees
Lies decaying on the lanes.

Above the keening rivulets
In the newly-dredged
Storm drains and ditches,
Suppurating gutters spill

Into a brimming rain butt,
Spurring on the puddles
With their persistent song,
While you and I hunker

In the steamed-up porch,
Stripping off our burdens –

These heavy jeans
That wick the equinox.

\*

When I see these shorelines in sight of each other –
The wader-wearing anglers on the far beach

Casting their weighted sand eels through the air
Into the deepest reaches of the inlet

And the fishermen on this nearside shore
Returning their lures in pendent arcs –

I see not just two towns estranged by water,
But two divergent settlements fused by flows:

The pier and shingle spit seen from the cliff,
The cliff and stocky lighthouse from the pier.

From what position do we observe a place?
Are we looking out, or looking in?

Upstream on the estuary's still mirror,
A pair of mute swans slowly tow their ghosts.

\*

Each day I turn up and make this sacrifice
*Sacri fice*   this making sacred
In oak, in bone, on leather. Scrolls.

*Runoz writu*   I cut the runes,
*Writu*   I hew, I write, I scribe,
A man who knows little but how

To colour the cold bed of letters:
The scratcher, the gouger,
Inscriber of gold,

Magician of snow and fire,
Observer of the wonders manifold,
Ritual worker, whalebone scribe,

The cultic reciter of oaken lore.
Incantor, I open
My magic song in the mouth of the world,

Leading the horse of my chisel
Across these sheets of bone,
To the barbershop lowing of cattle

Who graze outside my window on the bank
Where they have come in droves
To drink the sun.

*

From this sunken island
Uncovered twice each day
We watch the tack of ships,

The drift of seals and fish
In fluxes up-, down-stream,
Currents, tides, cormorants

And bright-beating egrets,
Terns pitching through the waves,
Bass on the turn of tides,

Chasing clouds of elvers
Under the flyover
With its river of cars…

And are ourselves observed
By the eyes of the past,
Of mackerel and trout

Chasing dense schools of fry
In the rough cross currents
At the estuary's mouth

Where the ferryboat's prow
Spears the opposite shore
As its fares disembark

Through the shallows and surf
To sit down in the sun
And drink an ice-cold beer.

## V. The High Barrow

*(right panel)*

ᚻᚷᚱᚻᛋᛋᛋᛇᛏᛦᚦᛋᛡᚻᛦᚱᛗᛒᚷᚱᚷᛦᚢᚷᛚ
ᛞᚱᛇᚷᛇᚦᛋᚹᛦ
ᚻᛇᚱᛇᚷᚱᛏᚢᚷᚷᛇᛋᚷᚱᚢᚠᛋᛦᚱᛞᛖᛡᛋᛋᚱᚷᛦᚢ
ᛡᛞᛋᚷᚠᚨᛏᛋᚱᛡᛦ
ᚱᛁᛋᚳᛁ
ᛒᛁᛏᚨ
ᚹᚢᛞᚢ

*Her Hos sitiþ on harmberga*
*agl drigiþ swa hiræ Ertae gisgraf*
*sarden sorga sefa torna.*
*risci / wudu / bita*

*Here Hos sits on the high barrow;*
*suffering distress as Ertae had imposed it,*
*a wretched den of sorrows and torments of mind.*
*rushes / wood / beast*

I time my scorper's strokes.
I chase the whalebone clear
Around the horse's head
As he waits by the mound,

Listening for the hooves
That ride through history;
Smelling the absent ghost
Of the whale's ambergris;

Scuffing my loose-shod feet
Through pared away fragments
That litter my cell's floor.

So, the mysteries speak
In sunlight through the lancet's glass.
My name is cut in ice.

\*


And then the hard-wearing inscriptions
Notched into the face of standing stones,

Devices carved in the cult of the dead
To protect the departed from thieves

And anchor them in place to halt their roving…
*To the glory of god… in memory of…*

A paleolithic jawbone unearthed
Among the flints and artefacts…

Names carved on stalactites in caves
That hang like ice from the gutter…

*William Petre 1571 was here*
*and Robert Hedges 1688…*

And on the township's cenotaph
In gold *Our Glorious Flanders Dead…*

\*

Down at the mouth of the river
The Newfoundland cod boats set sail
To satisfy demand for fish and land
Taken from the skraelings who know
How to fish their distant waters.

The boats pass by oncoming Danish raiders;
A hail of arrows over the harbour wall.
They pass Dunkirkers homeward bound;
Pass Flemish privateers and the French fleet
Who've landed here to plunder, burning altars.

Down on the shoreline, naked to the knee,
The Shaldon Amazons haul in their nets
And creel pots of willow and birch.
A muscled draft horse pulls their boats upshore
As their men disappear for the New World.

The oak posts of the beach groynes
Rise like spears to hold the water back –
All day it punches in with icy surf. From above
They are nothing more than feathers; from above
A pilot heads back to the aerodrome

On Little Haldon Hill, ruffling the slacks
Of the Sunday golfers patrolling the links,
Where the road runs through the hillfort,
A single scarp hidden by hedgebanks:
*Defnasburh, Deveneberie,* Fort of Devon's Folk.

\*

I sing the praise of the stand of oaks
   Handwritten against the horizon,

Their glyphs of twig and branch and stem
Scrawled across a winter sky;
I sing of the ciphers of horse hooves
Indented in the mud;
I sing the songbook of the spear
Whittling the air – the heron
Returning to the heronry
Through evening's stillness.
I sing the lyrics of ice and sun,
Whose teamwork brings
All rocks and stones to dust;
I sing the melody and rhythm of the chisel,
Fashioning the letters
On their journey of becoming.
Mine is the longhand of hardwood,
Of oak and ash whose branches join
Disparate times…
No one knows to where
Their hidden roots run;
I sing the valley-filling dew
Which comes back each day,
Gloriously green
Into the well of the world,
Where a traveller's horse stands bound,
A warden on the burial mound.

\*

Snatched from the creature's warmth
And brought into the sun,
I've made this voyage to artful box,
Honed and planed and realised
In six sheer sheets of ivory.
For months I knew the workman's hands

That hovered over each waiting face;
   His fingernails bitten and knuckles callused
Masking his exquisite artistry;
   How he handled the chisel and awl,
Sketched out horses and knights,
The spears of the besiegers,
The bricks of Jerusalem,
City sieges, she wolfs and suckling babes;
   How he cut the runes as though
He was sliding his kitchen knife
Through bread on an oaken board;
   Sitting up nights long after the sun
Had sunk, by candlelight,
In his *scriptorium*,
Until the day when all six sides
Were meshed together and I took up
My treasured hoard.
   I felt the pulse of his blood through his fingers
Like the beat of his horse's hooves,
His breath rich with wine and ambition
As though his very will
Was knocking at god's door.

*

In all these figures, filigree and knots –
In all this yielding bone that's swum across
Sea-lanes and history to a monk's refuge –
The ghosts we see, of course, are no such thing,
But simply what remembrance makes of them;
The laden look we witness on a stranger's face
That houses recollections of *our* dead.

We have the measure of our lives all wrong;
It's not this time of flesh and blood alone,
But the slow millennia of dissolution,
When skin and bone return to whence they came.
Do not detain me; lift the lid and give
These fragments back to the machinery
Of the world… this shared and ever constant now.

Lightning Source UK Ltd.
Milton Keynes UK
UKHW010959030619

343725UK00007B/104/P